How to Write

A

Family History

How to Write a Family History
And
Why you should

Ed McKie

First Published 2014

Second Edition Fully revised

© Ed McKie 2018

ISBN **ISBN:** 978-1-9802-2148-7

All the illustrations used in this book are the personal property of the author or in the public domain as far as it has been possible to establish.

Jeaned Books,
Warrington Cheshire

Contents

You Can I write a Family history..1
Why you should write a family history...................................2
How to begin..4
The past is a foreign country..9
People...11
Occupations..13
Accommodation...15
Places...17
Children, Schools and Work...21
Hospitals and the workhouse...22
Manner of death and who was left behind..........................23
World War one Connection..24
Photos and illustrations..26
Black sheep and sadness...28
Include Family stories...30
A matter of Style..31
Now for something completely different.............................33
Write a memoir..34
Now Come Back...38
Coming to a stop..39
Having a book printed..41

YOU CAN I WRITE A FAMILY HISTORY.

Most people, when it is suggested that they should put their family history research into a book, baulk at the idea. They consider that they are not writers, or that it would be too difficult and would involve a lot of extra work.

None of this is true. Consider how established authors of both fiction and non fiction work. For the most part, they research their subject thoroughly and then begin the writing process.

As a genealogist or family historian, whatever style you prefer, you are already half way there. You have done the research so it is just a question of writing it down.

How you write is only a question of style and it doesn't have to be done in any particular way. This is your book and you don't have to follow a format laid down by someone else.

The layout of your narrative is also a matter of personal preference, or with an eye to potential readership. It is quite possible to write a book which no-one else ever reads, however that should not be the aim. It is far better to have an audience in mind when writing. Think about your own descendants and that you want to tell them the story of what you have discovered about your ancestors. Not just the births deaths and marriages but the stories you have heard and what you have found about they way they lived. Write the story accordingly and you will find that it is a lot easier and better.

WHY YOU SHOULD WRITE A FAMILY HISTORY.

Having agreed that the writing of a family history is well within the capability of anyone who has had the determined effort of researching their ancestors then comes the other question of should they.

For most who have already gone down that road, there is no question, family histories need to be written. There are three main reasons for this and there may well be others:

FIRST: DON'T WASTE YOUR RESEARCH.

You have spent a lot of time and effort and perchance a fair bit of money in the process of finding out about your ancestors. It would be a great shame and a waste for it not to be recorded in a way that will be understandable to others, particularly those who no little of the processes of genealogical research. Not everyone is able to follow a gedcom or even a basic family tree if there are more than three or four generations. Your present day family, who, perhaps do not appear to be particularly interested at this time may well come to want to know about their ancestors in the future, and a book could be just the incentive they need.

SECONDLY: YOUR ANCESTORS DESERVE IT

Your great grandparents, or whichever part of your family you decide to focus on for your first book should not be left unheard of and unremembered. You have the capacity and the knowledge to make a record of their lives, so that future generations will know about them and regard them as real people in the way that you have become to during your research.

Finally no one else will do it

The chances are no-one else is going to write a book about your ancestors, so it is up to you. Not only can you do it, you should. Consider the alternatives, many years of work recorded in a gedcom on a CD, or a loose-leaf binder full of Family Group Sheets, Descendant charts and so on. Most regard that as being unsatisfactory compared to a printed book. Also consider that the digital age is changing so fast that it may well be your computerised records will not be readable in the future. The technology of the printed book is always going to be there and will never be superseded. Even if you only print a dozen or so books, there will always be a copy somewhere.

HOW TO BEGIN.

Perhaps the title of this chapter should be "When to begin". The answer to that is NOW.

Many how to do it books on a variety of skills include too many "don'ts". Not here! The emphasis is on the positive, *your book, your way* is the way I look at it and , of course, I think it is the only way.

Advice books for writers often suggest that you read a lot of other books of the same kind , the same genre in the jargon of publishing, to see how others have done it. This may well be useful in many instances, but for a family history it should not be the case. The opposite could be preferable. It does not matter in the slightest how other people have written family histories or biographies. This is your family story, your book and it is not a pot-boiler written to a formula learned at some writers workshop.

Do not be put off by the thought that you are not a professional writer, you do not need to be. Most non-fiction books, particularly of the academic kind are not written by professional writers, they are written by experts.

You are *the* expert in your chosen subject: your family. If you have been researching for a while then there will be few others who know more than you. If along the way you have come across cousins, distant or otherwise who are researching the same families as yourself then you can compare notes and you have extra expertise.

You have no doubt come across instances of facts that you do not agree on with other researchers. Do not shy away from that.

Recheck your own facts, then when you are sure that you are correct then you must accept a disagreement. Claim your facts and include it in your narrative but there is no harm in mentioning the different version. It adds to the story.

In *Alice in Wonderland*, "Begin at the beginning," the King said, very gravely, "*and go on till you come to the end: then stop*". It does not have to be quite like that, but it is not a bad premise to start with, and you could stick with it if you wish, many do.

Whilst the title of this book is "How to write a Family History" it is not a DIY Manual or a blueprint. I am of the opinion that there is no one way to write a family history. However, it is not a bad idea to have a plan at the beginning, even it it is only basic. Think perhaps of of those pieces of furniture that you buy that you have to put together yourself. You have all the pieces laid out on the floor and cannot understand a word of the instructions. It is a weekend and the supplier is not available so you just have to get stuck in and work it out.

Your research is your bits and pieces and you just assemble it in a way that make sense to you.

Another analogy is a jigsaw puzzle where you have all the pieces and have to make a picture.

A plan for your book could be just a list of headings or a complete layout.

Think of the main headings:

> *The People.*
>
> *The Place,*
>
> *The Events.*

Then write just short pieces under each of these headings to get yourself going. You do not have to think of them as book chapters in the beginning, that will come later.

Choose some ancestor, perhaps one set of great grandparents, make it easy on yourself and choose a pair which have something different about them for you to hang a story on.

You can decide on a format or layout, or you can leave that until later and just write chapters and juggle them around later. That is quite easy in most word processing programmes.

It is not necessary to think of chapters as they appear in fiction books. Chapters in a family history can be any length you like and of varying lengths, according to the parts of the story you are recording.

Births, marriages and deaths are the normal flow of most families lives, or perhaps that should be marriages, births and deaths, but that sequence is not always adhered to and never has been. It may be that this is not the best way of telling a story. However it can be helpful at the beginning to deal with those events in separate chapters but consider moving them about in the story when you have the words down.

It is difficult not to be boring when simply recounting the bare facts so a conscious effort needs to be made to avoid this. Most family historians are well aware of the glazed look of non aficionados when two researchers get together to discuss the latest finds. You don't want that glazed look coming over when someone is reading your book, especially if they have paid for it!

If there is some significant event in the lives of the couple you have chosen, consider starting with that, and then go on to tell the other things.

Choosing a period of time in a families lie can be another way of organising a narrative. If the family were on the 1861 census, an almost middle point in the Victorian era in England, then that could be be start of a story.

If the family includes someone who served in the armed forces in the first world war , then the 1911 census would be a good place to start. It is possible to go backwards and forwards in time in a story, it does not have to be consecutive.

Do not wait until you think your research is finished, that may never happen so write what you know now. There will be opportunities to add some more later if you come across new information, but more about that later.

Most people starting to compile a family tree have read the books which say start with yourself and work your way back. Nothing wrong with that, it is the standard way. So an ancestral chart is filled in: beginning with ourselves in a little box, drawing a line to two other little boxes and filling in the names of our parents. We then draw some more lines and add four boxes and fill in the names or our grand-parents. When we have done that, if we are not careful, we think of these people as individuals in little boxes. This is particularity true of the female halves of a couple. Once we have written down that the wife of William Jones was Mary Ann Smith, then it is easy to constantly think of her during the research as Mary Ann Smith, especially when looking for her parents.

No little boxes

BUT for the purposes of writing a family history it is essential to break out of thinking in this way – a modern phrase "think outside the box" is very apt.

Remember John Donne *"No man is an island"*. It is much more than not being an island it is remembering and writing that every person is not only an individual but is a member of a family. We are all individuals but we are part of a unit which is the family which is the focus of our story.

So a story could commence,

> "John and Mary lived in Connaught Street, Sutton in the Hole, where they had both lived all their lives"

Or

> "In 1861, at the time of the census, John and

> *Mary were living in Camberwell New Road, their third home since they were married five years previously."*

Something like this has got to be better than:

> *"John Evans was born on the 28th September 1832, the son of Peter Evans and Mary."*

The narrative should not be overloaded with too many dates. A list of descendants with all their dates can be included at the end of the book, in fact it is quite a good idea to do so, but they are not necessary in body of the story. If there is some particularly significant date which connects to another event, family or historical, then that can be included in the narrative in a natural way as being part of the story rather than the date being important in itself.

The Past is a Foreign Country.

In 1953, L.P. Hartley started his novel *"The Gobetween"* with those words and they have been quoted often since. It may not have been an original idea, but no matter.

It is a thought provoking idea and one needed to be kept in mind when writing a family history. Whilst not literally true, obviously, the way that the world changes, ever more frequently, it could almost be true.

Any 50 year old person today experienced things in their childhood which no longer exist in the every day world of modern living: telephone boxes, steam trains, home deliveries by the milkman etc. Go back a century and the list of such things is even longer. Couple that with things which are common today but which had not even been thought of a century ago, even in science fiction. The list for this is too long to make. Anything which requires the use of electronics or a microchip could not have been conceived of then, as even the use of electricity itself was only just being developed on any scale.

Keeping all of this in mind will help to fashion the story of a distant ancestor. Their lives were different without forgetting that as people, they essentials were still the same.

The fictional Victorian family, father going to work, mother staying home to look after the house, children saying "Yes Papa, No Mama" did not apply to everyone. The village shopkeeper and his family living over the shop had different lives to the Parson in the vicarage. They also lived differently to the carman who, with his horse and cart, delivered the goods to his shop. The stratas of society not only were clearer then, to a great extent they determined how people lived. The regularity and amount of income determined the standard of housing, the food on the table and the clothes that were worn. Housing and food influenced the health or otherwise of the family and often determined how long a child might live after birth.

Town and country lives were also a world apart. Many people living in rural villages had their horizons limited by the long distances between where they lived and the nearest town. Most would have required a compelling reason to make a long walk of perhaps several miles to visit a nearby market town when there was no transport available.

Whilst the separation of town and country is self evident the difference between poverty and wealth was also clear, but the shades in between were more subtle.

How these differences are dealt with in a family history narrative is a matter of choice and sometimes will be coloured by the view of social history held by the author. There is nothing wrong with including a personal view of how history may have impinged on the lives of a given set of ancestors, as long as the facts are clear enough to support a given point of view.

People

You may consider that you do not know sufficient about your chosen couple, but when you begin to put it down in a narrative form, then you will find that you know more than you realise.

You know where they were born and who their parents were and most likely the names and ages of siblings.

You may know where they went to school.

You will know the man's occupation and perhaps where he worked. Was it a trade? Was is it in a local factory, where many of their neighbours also worked. Check on history of local firms. Was he an "Ag Lab," if so which farm was it that he likely worked on.

You will know how many children they had, how many grew up to have families of their own and how many died in infancy.

Did the family stay together living in the same town or area or did they disperse at some stage? If the family parted ways at some point are there any indicators for the reasons. Did any of the children emigrate to Australia or Canada or some other. perhaps more exotic, place.

Were there uncles and aunts and cousins living nearby or far away. Were they visited or did they appear to be estranged. What about the parents, did they live to good ages or were all of them dead before the marriage of your chosen couple?

Most of this information is already in your records, but does not appear in that way in your Group sheets if you use that format.

Most researchers are now using genealogical computer programmes to record their research and they are generally regarded as being essential. Certainly after a few years, filling in Family Group sheets in loose-leaf folders becomes totally impractical.

However from the point of view of writing a family history, a drawback of many genealogical programmes is that they are designed to regard the individual as being in a box and joined to other individuals who are also in a box.

Writers of family histories have to break out of thin king in that way. It is a good idea to print out a Family Group Sheet from your genealogy programme and keep it on your desk. Having this in the forefront whilst writing will remind you that it is the whole family that it is the subject of the story not just one individual.

It is also useful to create a timeline for both individuals of a couple. Many family tree programmes can do that, otherwise it is not difficult to create one from the Group Sheets.

A timeline can help to plot the life passage as it were, to see where events slot one into another. As an example a timeline will point up where your focus couple were when their first child married: were they still in the family home? or had they moved on? Were there younger siblings still at home? All these aspects help to build up a picture, and a picture of their lives is what you are wanting to create in your book.

OCCUPATIONS

It must be borne in mind that even if the past is not exactly a foreign country, occupations have changed down the years. The names, in many instances, have remained the same, but the job itself has changed.

A carpenter in the early 19th century was doing a completely different job to anyone being called a carpenter in the 21st century.

You may well also have come across occupations that no longer exist. From the storytelling point of view, be glad of that. Most family historians would love to have a "saggermakers bottom knocker" in the family. Although you may not come across anything so bizarre, there are still many 19th century occupations, common at that time, which no longer exist in any real sense today. Domestic service for instance is not what it was, nor is the agricultural labourer the jack of all trades required by farmers in the past. Most of the occupations and trades related to the enormous use of horses both in the country and in the town have

also gone. Metal work that was done by hand is now fully mechanised and anyone carrying out work formerly done by a blacksmith will be working in a factory today instead of in a small workshop.

The printing trade no longer requires a man to set lead type by hand to be put in a machine to have ink rolled over it. Your digital camera no longer requires the services of someone to process film and to print out the resultant photographs in a darkroom.

And so the list will go on and it is necessary to look at the occupations seen on a census with an eye to understanding what those particular jobs entailed at that time. A typewriter for instance at one time was a person not a machine, a carman worked with horse-drawn vehicles before the advent of the internal combustion engine and an engine driver could easily refer to a man working in a factory rather than on the railway.

From all over the country there are trades no longer required. No stocking knitters in Derbyshire, no leather dressers in South London, no ostlers at the wayside pub to look after the horses of travellers. There is the modern day equivalent of the stage coach, of course, hurtling up the motorways at 60 miles per hour, but no one is required to blow a horn to have a turnpike opened if they are carrying mail.

Accommodation

It is not always easy to to deduce what kind of housing accommodation any given family was occupying from a single census.

However, it can often be worked out by looking at a series of censuses for the same street. From 1851 onwards each family on the schedule was quite clear, and house end was clearly marked. So that from looking at the entries for several houses in a street it can show, how many were in multiple occupation and how many had only the one household present.

A hundred years ago, for most working families, in most towns, rents were such that they had to make do with fewer rooms than would be regarded as being sufficient today. A man needed to have a steady, regularly well paid job in order to be able to afford to rent a whole house for his family. Most just had a few rooms in a house shared with one or more other families.

Housing, like so many other things varied from place to place and from period to period. Town and country differed, suburb to suburb in the town was different. A country cottage with a thatched roof can look quaint on the lid of a box of chocolates, however once inside the low lintelled front door (a reminder that generally folk were quite a bit shorter than today) the prospect is different. Dirt floors in older cottages were not uncommon and often there was only one room with a similar sized one above. No cooking stoves or indoor bathroom and mostly no piped water.

In the towns, back to back houses were always overcrowded by today's standards. Quite large families often lived in two rooms, and censuses often reveal that in addition to the families themselves there were frequently lodgers.

Up until the middle of the nineteenth century, artisans houses in towns rarely had an indoor water supply and never an indoor toilet. Try to imagine how that affected the way people lived. Clearly there was little privacy for anything. Perhaps difficult to imagine today, but the writer needs to.

Places

Whether it be town or village, these days it is not difficult to get descriptions of places as they were in the past. If not of actual streets, then a nearby street could be similar or the neighbourhood may well have to do, but it all helps to put the family into a context that will make it possible for readers to appreciate what life was like at a particular point in time.

If it is not possible to visit a place which will appear in a history, then *Google earth* (https://www.google.co.uk/intl/en_uk/earth) can be a useful substitute. Looking at a place as it is now, is not necessarily going to be useful to visualise what it was like a century or so ago, but many places still have vestiges of what they were, and a surprising number of villages have not changed substantially.

One building which has a strong likelihood of still looking as it was all those years ago is the Parish Church. If you have a baptism record then a photo of the church is a nice illustration to add to your pages, and a photo of the font itself, additionally so.

The places where people lived were not just an abode, but they will have influenced their lives as well, and it is useful to consider that and make it part of the story. Even if the children of a family were christened in the local Anglican parish church, that does not say that they were regular churchgoers. In pre-civil registration days, many who were not regular churchgoers still took their children to the church as a form of legal acknowledgement of family lines.

The censuses carried out in Britain every ten years are a mine of information not just for the researcher but for the family historian as well. It is very easy to slip into the habit of regarding the census page containing the household details as being all there is that needs to be recorded. Nothing could be further from the truth. As previously said most people live not just in families but in neighbourhoods. The neighbours also influenced their lives in the same way that they do today, but even more so.

Most are aware that prior to the first world war, even people living in towns were more connected to their neighbours than they are today. People considered themselves safer then so that open front doors were the norm more than otherwise. Neighbours dropped in to borrow or to chat. Friends helped with illness and with childbirth and at the end, quite often it was a neighbour he assisted with the "laying out" of a dead person.

Obviously the census is not going to record how any individual family related to their neighbours, but it does tell us who those neighbours were and an examination of the whole street and the adjoining ones will give a flavour of the area, how many different occupations there were, if the married women needed to work, were the youngsters apprenticed or just errand boys or shop-girls. Children were often described as "scholars" but that is no guarantee that they actually attended school. Keeping an eye out for familiar names on a census can show that often neighbours were in fact relatives.

Country areas are much easier to deal with on the census, because it is comparatively easy to view and make a list of everyone in a village, and relationships much more easily identified.

The census from 1851 onwards also lists the place of birth of everyone in the household (or it should do). It is clear then that if children in the family had different places of birth, then the family had moved at some time in between, which gives another location to look at and to include in the narrative. It is also interesting to consider why these moves took place, particular if it was in an area where normally families remained for many years. Some historical event may have taken place to make a move imperative.

Whilst it is not possible to walk down a street of 1861 it is possible to visualise and to describe. Picture postcards of many places exist and are available on line or from a local history library. Social media are also a useful source of old picture postcards. These old postcards usually do not just show old buildings but also people so are also useful as reminders of clothes at the time when the card was published.

Even if you can't reproduce the picture in your book for copyright reasons, you can still use it. Prop up a picture postcard of an area and look at it as if you were looking through a window. Describe what you would see if you actually walked along the street. Mention the shop as you went by, the name over the fascia, the goods in the window. Mention the vehicles on the road and describe the pedestrians, if there are any, what they were wearing, ages and so on. From this you can provide colour and body to your story.

Don't forget to explain those things which you consider may not be familiar to your readers. Not everyone will know what cobble stones are, or what gas lamps looked like or indeed how they were lit.

All those things that were familiar to your forbears, and which are for the most part, long forgotten now. Remind your readers about them.

Do not forget to include the sounds. Obviously you can not hear the sounds from a postcard, but you do know that the things that you can see in the picture will probably be making some noise. The sound of horses hooves as they draw carts with iron rimmed wheels over stone roads is completely different to the sound of rubber tyres on tarmac. Horses also often carried jingling brasses on their collars which added to the street noise. Is there a street seller in your picture or might their have been one just round the corner, what would the be calling out. The time on a street clock might indicate if the church bells would have been ringing then. Conversations would be going on between the folk in the street, then as now, except that no one would be talking an a mobile phone.

CHILDREN, SCHOOLS AND WORK.

Whilst your focus is generally on your couple and their family and I have shown a preference for regarding them as a unit rather than as individuals, they are still individuals.

This applies even more so to the children in the family. The adults have lives centred around work and home, but children in the past were no different in many respects to children today. They are part of the family but have lives of their own. Quite often secret lives that their parents are only partly unaware of.

Children were often listed on the censuses as scholars without actually attending school.

Although school attendance became compulsory in England in 1870 for all children between the ages of 5 and 10, it did not apply to children who were already at work.

Children regularly started work at an early age and the scandal of child workers in factories is well known. Check to see if there was a factory in the area where your family lived to see if they employed young children.

There are some school attendance registers available on line but they are mainly for the later part of the nineteenth century, however it is worthwhile to check to see they exist for the children of your families.

Hospitals and the Workhouse

As is well known the fear of the workhouse for unemployed and destitute poor in the nineteenth century was real and often for good reason.

There are records available in many repositories and some are available on line. The only hospital in many areas was the infirmary attached to the local workhouse, so that the sick are often included in records marked "workhouse" when in fact they have gone into the local infirmary.

Children were also taken into the childrens' ward of the workhouse when their parents were in the infirmary. A form of being taken into care but mostly this was just short term.

The infirmary records are also often a source of information about the cause of death and how long an individual had been in the hospital before dyeing.

If you have family who are shown in any of these records then it gives another illustration of how their lives were managed. A death certificate will record a date, place and cause of death, but when it is at an early age there is no explanation. The hospital records can reveal this.

MANNER OF DEATH AND WHO WAS LEFT BEHIND

The bare facts of births, marriages and deaths coupled with the census entries can help to fill out details of family life, if looked at with a fresh eye, and a modicum of imagination.

Which of the couple was the first one to die and how did the survivor cope? Were some of the children still young, death in childbirth was an all too common occurrence. Had some of the older children already married and moved away or where they still living nearby?. If the couple or just one of them survived into old age, how would they have manage financially? Did they need to carry on working till the end or were they able to sit back somewhere and be looked after? Would the grandchildren have been able to visit or were they too far away?

Then finally, where did they die and where buried? Was there a will? Wills are so useful, but unfortunately all too many ancestors had nothing worth leaving so a will was not considered necessary.

However, do not regard the death of one or both of the ancestor couple as being the end of the story. See how the children stayed or dispersed. Did any follow the same occupation as the father?. Did the girls make successful marriages? Were there many grand children or few?

World War One Connection

If an ancestor served or even died in the first world war then the centenary, provides an incentive to write his story. Even if this does not apply to the husband of your focus couple, then perhaps one or even several of the sons could have served between 1914 and 1918.

Learn about Regiments and battles they were or could have been involved in. There is no need for a history of the Great War it has already been done, but how the war and its consequences affected your family should be part of your story.

If one of the so-called "Pals Battalions" were raised in the vicinity of where an ancestor lived, even if one did not join, the fact that many neighbours and their sons did so affected the families around. The arrival of the inevitable telegrams and letters advising of dead or missing soldiers impinged on the lives, not just of those receiving them, but of their friends and neighbours also.

The 1911 census, readily available on line in many places, including perhaps a local library is a mine of information about the men who fought and in many instances died, in the war.

The young men who died perhaps in 1917, for the most part were still at school in 1911, others were apprentices. The young married men were with new wives and first babies. Did their occupations prepare them for the military lives they were to follow in only a few short years after the taking of the census. Even if they were in manual jobs, it was no guarantee, given the endemic poverty of the time, that any would necessarily been fitter than the young clerk in an office.

Whilst large numbers of the service records of soldiers in world war one were destroyed in a bombing raid in World war two, there are still some records which can help.

The Commonwealth War Graves Commission website contains a list of all those who died with sometimes information about relatives. The National Archives also has a searchable database of the Medal records from which one can learn of many soldiers' regiment.

Once knowing the regiment of an individual soldier it is possible, with the publication of the "War Diaries" by the National Archives in 2014, to read about what a given unit was doing during the course of the war. These are handwritten records, but some have been transcribed, and in both instances than can be difficult but revealing reading. Few ordinary soldiers are mentioned in the war diaries and often the smaller units such as companies are also not identified, however much of the information contained can be woven into a family history story. Not just to tell a story, but to ensure that it is not forgotten.

Photos and Illustrations

Many family historians regret that they do not have any photographs of anyone older say than their grandparents. This unfortunately if true for the vast majority. However that should not be deterrent to including illustrations in a family history book. If photographs of family members are available then they should be included, but failing that there are other illustrations which can be used

Photos and drawings of the places which appear in the narrative of the story can often be found, either from tourist board sites or from old postcards which have been published on the internet. There are also numerous illustrations available which can be used to show what people wore, what traffic was like along local streets and well known figures from the same locality all add colour to the story without necessarily being your family. +

There is the need to take care with copyright but there are many thousands of public domain photographs and drawings available, which can be used, so there is no need to risk copyright infringement.

If there are photographs of unidentified people make that clear with a caption and the same with places, if you have a picture of a place on a page about another place, then make that clear also.

There is no need to risk confusing the reader.

The old saw "a picture is worth a thousand words" may not apply to family history books, but pictures are useful to illustrate words which are describing places and things which are no longer seen in everyday life.

Most followers of the television series "Dr. Who" will be familiar with a Police Box, but few under middle age would have seen one in the street. And so it is with so many things which can be brought to life in a family history narrative to show the look of previous times.

Horse-drawn vehicles are no longer the familiar sight that they were many years ago and an illustration of a traffic jam involving this type of vehicle could be juxtaposed with a modern street scene.

It is unnecessary to fill the book with unrelated illustrations but a look at any book on local history and the like will show that a judiciously placed illustration makes the world of difference in an otherwise solid block of text.

This book for instance would have a completely different look without the few illustrations that are included.

BLACK SHEEP AND SADNESS.

Many family historians have come across instances of suicide or prison sentences amongst their forbears. Some will consider that the recording of events that occurred more than a hundred years ago, cannot hurt anyone living today, whilst others have a different point of view. To record that an ancestor committed an offence and went to prison, or another committed suicide or that a young woman had a baby out of wedlock, should not be a matter of shame for anyone living today.

Everyone will deal with these things differently, but do not shy away from anything like this if they occur in your family.

These events need to be dealt with sensitively but they should not be omitted from the family story. They are what happened and they will have had an impact on the family which could be explored in a narrative.

Australian researchers these days are as pleased as punch to find that one of their ancestors was brought before a judge at the Old Bailey and transported to Van Diemens land. Not everyone is going to take a similarly sanguine view of the misdeeds of distant ancestors, but it is better not to judge, just to try to understand how it was that these events took place.

The somewhat trite phrase about the past being a foreign country should not be taken too literally when it comes to considering people. A much more apt phrase is "folk are folk" and it is much more likely that our great grand-parents were people much like ourselves. They lived and laughed in much they same way that people do today, met misfortune in the best way that they could and even if they did not achieve happiness, the chances are that they did no harm to anyone.

INCLUDE FAMILY STORIES

Most families have stories which have been handed down through generations. Many of them are unprovable for a variety of reasons, but they can be used in the narrative of a family history book, making clear that they are family fables.

If you have not been able to identify a member of a family on a census, or find their marriage or death on the indexes, that it may well be true that they emigrated to Canada or wherever. Or perhaps an Aunt did not "run off with the milkman", she may have just entered into a common law relationship with a man whose name she adopted.

Discussing these possibilities in a family history may help someone following on, to pick up the threads and perhaps find, through later published records, the missing piece of evidence, which in the past has been elusive.

The massive movement of populations over the years and the consequent splitting of families has meant that many personal family records have been lost, and the memories of what occurred has been passed down in haphazard manner which often obscures the truth. It is therefore imperative that whatever snatches of story that exist, should be recorded and the truth or otherwise left to be discovered.

A Matter of Style

You can read as many books as you like on how to write and most will not help you in the slightest. This book is not about telling you how to write but I hope that along the way there have been some pointers about things to include. I said at the beginning there were not going to be "don'ts" however here I am going to suggest a few.

In my early family history books I wanted to be factual and if I did not know something but assumed it then I would cover myself by using words like "perhaps" or "most likely " and so on.

Since then I have decided that this was not really necessary, and you may feel the same. For instance if there was only the one school in a village then I now think that it is not necessary to say "George would have attended the local school" or "it is likely that George attended the local school". I think that it is enough to say that "There was only the one school in the village...."

The same with accommodation. If you don't have an address then just describe the types of accommodation in the vicinity without attempting to guess at what kind your ancestor lived in.

One of my ancestors was an oilman and there was a local paint factory two streets away so I wrote that William probably worked in that factory. That was unnecessary guesswork and I could have just included that fact of his occupation and the proximity of a possible employer.

This approach may not commend itself to you, but if it does you will find that a lot of obvious presumptions and guesses can be avoided. You will also avoid paragraphs which only look like padding.

I have suggested a simple narrative style here but there are alternatives which commend themselves to many writers. Creative fiction and a short story format are two of them.

If you have the imagination for it then a creative fiction version of your family history has much to commend it. You will probably satisfy readers who seek dialogue in their reading but you will also disappoint some who want a true story.

A short story format is also useful if you have difficulty with maintaining a flowing narrative style. A bit like a blog, a book of relatively short chapters each telling of a single incident or event can be a way of overcoming that difficulty.

Now for something completely different

Ed McKie

WRITE A MEMOIR.

Most family historians will agree that much research over the years has been made more difficult because forbears did not leave a diary or write a memoir. Often the best that can be hoped for is a few entries in the back of a family bible.

How much easier it would have been if you had found a series of diaries in the attic, or even a bundle of letters. So much information about our ancestors has been lost because they didn't leave a record.

Have you learned a lesson from this and keep a diary or journal? Have you written a memoir?

If not, then start now.

It does not have to be a full blown autobiography. Unless you have lived a very interesting life, gone round the world three times, competed in the Olympics or whatever, an autobiography can be boring. Consider how many biographies fill the shelves of the second hand book shops, clearly only partially+ read. There is a limit to the interest you can maintain when writing *"My life in Kenya"* (with apologies to "As time goes by") and *"The day I scored the winning goal"* doesn't even last till the end of the match, let alone the end of the book.

Many life stories are begun in the belief that offspring and later generations would one day be interested. However the realisation soon sets in that it is going to take more time and effort than most are prepared to spend on this perhaps forlorn hope.

Blogging is an alternative.

Short pieces about various bits and pieces of interesting items come across during research. Short (they can be very short) stories about some aspect of an ancestors life, amusing stories that father had told about his time in the services and when he was young.

This is an alternative way of dealing with the writing of a memoir. No starting off with "I was born in the workhouse" and going on from there, but just a book of short stories. Much easier to write and more chance of being reasonably interesting and therefore read.

Everyone has stories about their youth and growing up, marriage and early married life, trials and tribulations and how they were overcome. This is life for most people and everyone deals with them differently and in years to come your grandchildren and their children will want to know about that.

Even though generally people are living longer, there are not going to be many fortunate enough to survive so their great-grandchildren will know them as people, rather than just a name, sometimes mentioned.

So why not start a blog, either on the net, or just on your hard drive. Write a story once a week, first day at school, first job, first kiss, whatever. What was your parents living room like. The house, the street, the neighbours. All of these are worth, say 500 hundred words. Don't make them too long. But within six months you will have a book, mishmash or pot-pourri it doesn't matter.

You will have written something which you can then use to have printed. You do not have to put them up for sale or even give them out willy nilly if you do not want to, but you will have done it and it will be worthwhile. Adding photos with everyone in them properly named will help to ensure that it all fits together. You will leave an inheritance much more important than anything you can include in your will, which will be treasured in years to come.

Try it now!!

Go to your computer, sit yourself comfortably and write 500 words about yesterday, or perhaps the weekend. That cant be too hard, can it? It was only yesterday or a couple of days ago and you cant have forgotten. Good day or bad day, doesn't matter, write it down and then you will have made a start. Just remember it does not have to be "literature" just you writing a letter to an old friend you have not seen for a while.

Next time you are on a social media, facebook or whatever, instead of just filling in your thought for the day, having a moan about something, go to your blog instead.

Then think about:

Earliest memories. What is the earliest event that you can remember and can you date it accurately?

Differences that you can see in your surroundings between now and then.

Things that no longer happen.

Things which did not exist then, mobile phones, cars for every household etc.

Food. How differently did you eat when you were young? Is your favourite food the same now as it was then? Are there foods you can no longer buy and conversely are there items which are now a regular part of your diet which you did not, or could not eat in these days gone by.

Clothing. How different are the clothes that you wear now? Not just in the fashion sense but in terms of materials.

Toys. How different were the toys you had compared to children of today?

Transport. Did you go to school or work by tram or bus?

Work. Your first job and what it entailed. How is the same job done today.

Wages. What did you earn in your early days and how does that compare with today taking into account inflation.

Once you have started recording your earlier life in this blogging fashion, then look again at the family history book you have also been writing. You will realise that the same thinking can be applied to that and it may well be the style that you come to prefer in writing the lives of your ancestors.

You may well decide that instead of aiming for a narrative form of a single novel like book it could well be a book of short stories. Each of these forms are equally valid in recording family history.

Ed McKie

Now Come Back

Coming to a Stop

Professional writers often suffer from writers block or some other reason why there is a struggle to continue. This is normal and all have different ways of overcoming this.

You may find that if you have taken the break suggested earlier and started to blog a memoir and now come back and cant get going again on your story. For family historians, a simple but effective means is often suggested. Start another story.

This may seem bizarre, but the thing to do with family histories that are stuck for whatever reason, is to start writing another. Bearing in mind that there are four sets of great grand-parents, then naturally there are four families to write about. At least one set, if not more, will be from a different place to the others, perhaps from a different income group and occupation, then their story will have a different setting.

Setting out to write a different story will help to keep the writing activity going, and will no doubt spark ideas for a new chapter or more in the original book.

It is not impossible to write two family history books in tandem, and many have found this is the simplest way of dealing with two different families, and helps to maintain a coherent style.

There is no need to worry over-much about repeating parts of the narrative already used in one book in the second if the time periods and the families overlap. The stories are going to be in two separate books and even if later they are combined into one, then the repetition will not be a significant drawback. The families are all essentially one and it is inevitable that things which were significant to part of a family are equally significant to another. No great lengths need to be taken to completely rewrite an episode for inclusion in another book. Regular readers of fiction will be familiar with established authors constantly referring back to events occurring in previous books of a series or having the same protagonist.

The important thing is not to give up. Try to set yourself a time for writing and if you are the really organised type set yourself a deadline for finishing just like writers who need to earn a living from their work. Letting the book drift along will let the time go by and you will then fear that you will not finish it. That is the first step to giving up. Tell all your relatives that you are writing this book and they will encourage you by constantly asking how it is coming along. Trust me! That will happen and it is an excellent incentive to keep going, you will not want to admit that you can't do it.

There are many causes of happiness in our lives and I am not going to try to compare this endeavour or its result to any of them. But the feeling when you come to hold that first printed book in your hand with your name on the cover is probably only surpassed by when you hold your first baby in your arms.

HAVING A BOOK PRINTED.

What to do with your final manuscript when it is finished. There is no point in all this work if it is going to be left sitting on a hard drive or just a few copies printed off on your home printer and handed around to some relatives.

You would be quite right in thinking that without getting some printed or having them printed would be a waste of all the effort. But it is not difficult to have a book published and printed so that you do not have to bear the cost of giving your books away.

It will of course depend on your expectations on what you would like your book to look like. Do you want a hard cover book like you see in a library or would a paper back be sufficient. Hard covers are more expensive to produce than paper backs and would obviously last a lot longer.

Print on demand publishing is a perfectly respectable way of dealing with your final manuscript. Not vanity publishing which can be expensive but print on demand and sales through the likes of Amazon can cost very little or even nothing at all.

What you will end up with in this process can be an attractive printed and bound record of your research and your family. Something which you can be proud of having produced and which your own descendants and others will recognise as being the result of work well done.

When you have that first printed volume in you hand you will without doubt turn to another pair of ancestors perhaps from a different part of the country or a different period in time and start on the second book.

Another great advantage of print on demand is that it is so easy to update a book, even after it is printed. Most researchers, no matter what age they get to, all keep having another bang at a brick wall or whatever you call those dead ends. With more and more information becoming available on the internet, archives publishing digitised records you will never know when that last little piece of the jigsaw which is our ancestors lives, will fall into place.

With print on demand it is easy to add an extra chapter, rewrite a paragraph or two or just add an addendum, without having to change anything else. And then publish a revised edition, it really is as easy as that.

There are several print on demand publishers for the UK author:

Createspace- an Amazon company

Blurb

Epubli

Xlibris

Writers World.

Other publishers are available in Europe and USA.

Details of the services that each of these publishers offer are easily found on their websites, and the time spent in investigating their charges and services is worthwhile.

They each have their attractions and downsides for any given author. The upfront costs vary from nothing in the case of Createspace to an open-ended figure with Writers World.

It is obvious that if you want to go for a no cost (apart from printing) then you will have to do the bulk of the work yourself. This is not as daunting as it may sound and it would be an interesting exercise in any case to try to do it yourself in the first instance.

If at the end of the exercise you find you cannot do it all yourself, then at least you will have a good idea of the aspects of the job that you are going to need help with.

Printed in Great Britain
by Amazon